ι ℓιι

D1202048

DOROTHY
DANDRIDGE

DOROTHY DANDRIDGE

SINGER & ACTRESS

by DeAnn Herringshaw

Content Consultant:
Charlene Regester, PhD, Department of African and
Afro-American Studies, University of North Carolina, Chapel Hill

ABDO
Publishing Company

CREDITS

Published by ABDO Publishing Company, 8000 West 78th Street, Edina, Minnesota 55439. Copyright © 2011 by Abdo Consulting Group, Inc. International copyrights reserved in all countries. No part of this book may be reproduced in any form without written permission from the publisher. The Essential Library™ is a trademark and logo of ABDO Publishing Company.

Printed in the United States of America,
North Mankato, Minnesota
112010
012011

 THIS BOOK CONTAINS AT LEAST 10% RECYCLED MATERIALS.

Editor: Rebecca Rowell
Copy Editor: Susan Freese
Interior Design and Production: Emily Love
Cover Design: Kazuko Collins

Library of Congress Cataloging-in-Publication Data
Herringshaw, DeAnn, 1962-
  Dorothy Dandridge : singer & actress / by DeAnn Herringshaw.
     p. cm. -- (Essential lives)
  Includes bibliographical references and index.
  ISBN 978-1-61714-779-1
  1. Dandridge, Dorothy, 1922-1965--Juvenile literature. 2. Motion picture actors and actresses--United States--Biography--Juvenile literature. 3. African American motion picture actors and actresses--Biography--Juvenile literature. 4. Singers--United States--Biography--Juvenile literature. I. Title.
  PN2287.D256H47 2011
  791.430'28092--dc22
  [B]
                              2010042150

TABLE OF CONTENTS

Dorothy Dandridge arrives at the Century Theater in New York City on March 30, 1955, for the Academy Awards.

A Symbol of Hope

The Academy Awards ceremony—also known as Oscar night—has been the biggest event in Hollywood since 1929. Nearly everyone in the movie business wants to win an Oscar, and simply being nominated is a great honor. So, when Dorothy

Dandridge was nominated for the Best Actress Oscar for her portrayal of Carmen in the 1954 film *Carmen Jones*, she was ecstatic. She was making film history, too.

Dandridge was the first African American—male or female—to be nominated for an Oscar in a starring role. To make Oscar night even more historic, Dandridge was to present the Academy Award for Best Film Editing, making her the first African-American woman ever to participate on stage in the prestigious awards ceremony. It was an important night for Dandridge, and her hopes and dreams were riding high—not only for herself and her career but for the progress of blacks everywhere.

The Academy

The Academy of Motion Picture Arts and Sciences has presented the Academy Award of Merit since 1929. Most people know the award by its nickname, Oscar, but no one knows for sure how it got this moniker. According to legend, when the academy librarian first saw the statue, she said it looked like her Uncle Oscar—and the name stuck. The academy does much more than hand out film awards every year. It also holds the Nicholl Fellowships in Screenwriting, a competition described as "the world's most esteemed screenwriting competition."[1]

For many African Americans watching the ceremony on television that spring night in 1955, Dandridge was a symbol of hope. Here was one of their own, a gorgeous, gifted, and gutsy woman, fighting for her place in Hollywood—a world dominated by white men. So many people wanted her to win, but even if she did not, she would still gain visibility that night—for herself and for all African Americans. And she would make a name for herself as one of the first African-American movie stars. If Dandridge could break the color barrier in Hollywood, integration for the rest of the nation would perhaps follow.

A Rising Star

It looked as though Dandridge was on her way to the top of the film industry. *Carmen Jones* was a box-office hit, and she had captured the character of the fiery, free-spirited Carmen perfectly. Her outstanding performance in the film had been the talk of

---

Hattie McDaniel

Actress Hattie McDaniel was the first African American to win an Academy Award. In 1940, she was presented the Oscar for Best Supporting Actress for her portrayal of the subservient "Mammy" in the 1939 film *Gone with the Wind.* She was also the first African American to attend the Academy Awards ceremony as a guest. McDaniel was invited to come on stage to accept her award, but she was not invited to dine with the white nominees. She had to sit at a segregated table in the back of the room.

Although a talented actress and singer, McDaniel's contract limited her to playing servant roles: slaves, maids, or cooks. Many people in the African-American community criticized her for reinforcing racial stereotypes, to which she gave this now famous response: "I'd rather play a maid for $700 per week than to be one for $7 per week."[2]

Since McDaniel's win, only three other African-American women have received the award: Whoopi Goldberg as Oda Mae Brown in *Ghost* (1990), Jennifer Hudson as Effie White in *Dreamgirls* (2006), and Mo'Nique as Mary Jones in *Precious* (2009).

Tinseltown for months. Dandridge had all the makings of a superstar: remarkable beauty, perfect poise, a startling presence, a lovely voice, and tons of talent. When she walked into a room, people stared. Because of her rare combination of beauty, grace, and spirit, people reacted to her the way they reacted to Elizabeth Taylor, Ava Gardner, and Marilyn Monroe. Dandridge knew she was just as good as any of the top white actresses and deserved a place among these stars.

When Dandridge arrived in a limousine with her sister, Vivian, and stepped out on the red carpet the night of the Oscars, she was dazzled. Journalists crowded the ropes on both sides of the red carpet, calling her name and asking for comments. Photographers flocked around her, their flashbulbs bursting as they snapped dozens of photos. And Dandridge, in her yellow satin gown, was the very picture of poise and sophistication. She seemed to be enjoying all the attention, but Vivian and a few close friends knew how frightened she really was.

The nominee was very nervous. She was going up against some of the brightest female stars in Hollywood. The four other nominees in the category were Judy Garland for *A Star Is Born*, Audrey Hepburn for *Sabrina,* Grace Kelly for *The Country Girl*, and Jane Wyman for *Magnificent Obsession*. Although Dandridge believed in herself and in her talent, she also had moments of overwhelming anxiety and crippling fear. She was so worried about losing in front of everyone that she probably would not have attended the ceremony if she had not been asked to present an award.

Dandridge hinted at the importance of this moment when it was her turn to present. She glided gracefully up to the podium. When she spoke, she did not try to hide her emotions. "If I seem a little nervous," she said into the microphone, "this is as big a moment for me as it will be for the winner of this award."[3]

Sidney Poitier

Sidney Poitier was the first African American to win the Best Actor Oscar for his work in *Lilies of the Field* (1963). As of 2010, only three other African-American actors have won this award: Denzel Washington for *Training Day* (2001), Jamie Foxx for *Ray* (2004), and Forest Whitaker for *The Last King of Scotland* (2006).

AND THE WINNER IS . . .

After presenting the award for film editing, Dandridge returned to her seat next to Vivian to wait for her category to be announced. Dandridge wanted to win more than anything, and she knew her performance in *Carmen Jones* was Oscar-worthy.

Grace Kelly accepted the Best Actress Oscar at the 1955 Academy Awards.

Still, she doubted whether the Academy of Motion Picture Arts and Sciences would really give her the award. Longtime friend and manager Earl Mills remembered Dandridge saying, "It's too soon for me to win. I'm too new in the movie business. If I don't win, I hope my friend Judy [Garland] wins it."[4]

When the Oscar for Best Actress was awarded, it went to Kelly. Dandridge was terribly disappointed for herself and for Garland. When the ceremony was over, she did not want to attend any of the Oscar parties she had been invited to. All she wanted to do was return to her quiet hotel room and rest.

Although Dandridge was disappointed she had not won an Academy Award, she was also somewhat relieved. Now that she was not under so much pressure to win, she could focus on building her career. She had worked long and hard as an entertainer and had come so far. She had endured hardships and humiliation from bigoted bigwigs in the entertainment business who had made her life difficult simply because she was not white.

But that all appeared to be behind her now. Her reputation as an accomplished actress was well established, and Hollywood was taking her seriously. Offers for more wonderful film roles would pour in, she thought, giving her many more choices and chances to win. Someday, she was certain, she would win an Oscar—all she needed was the opportunity.

Halle Berry

Seven African-American actresses have been nominated for the Best Actress Oscar, but as of 2010, only one had ever won this prize: Halle Berry, for her performance as Leticia Musgrove in *Monster's Ball* (2001). During Berry's acceptance speech, she held up her Oscar statue and said, "This is for Dorothy Dandridge."[5]

Hattie McDaniel, pictured in 1941, was the first African American to win an Academy Award when she won for best supporting actress in 1940.

Dorothy spent her early childhood in Cleveland, Ohio.

WONDER CHILD

Ruby Jean Butler was a tall, big-boned, and rowdy girl who loved to socialize and be the center of attention. Ruby was born in 1899. When she was in her late teens, she left her hometown of Wichita, Kansas, and moved to

Cleveland, Ohio, looking for opportunities to perform on stage.

In Cleveland, Ruby met Cyril Dandridge, a slender, handsome, and gentle young man. Cyril worked as a mechanic and draftsman and was devoted to his mother, Florence, a respectable and proper lady. Cyril's dream was to have a quiet, secure life in his hometown and to keep his mother happy.

Ruby and Cyril were married on September 30, 1919, and began having problems right away. Cyril brought Ruby to live in the comfortable home he shared with his mother, but Ruby and her mother-in-law did not get along. Florence thought Ruby was loud and sloppy. Ruby thought Florence was demanding and critical. Ruby often called Cyril a "mama's boy" because he always did what his mother wanted.

Broken Home

In April 1921, Ruby gave birth to a little girl whom she and Cyril named Vivian. Ruby was now a mother. Even so, the energetic, freedom-loving Ruby could not be the obedient housewife Cyril and Florence wanted her to be. Two months after Vivian was born, Ruby packed up, took the baby, and left

Cyril. After she had been gone for six weeks, Cyril found Ruby and convinced her to come home. Ruby did return home, but she and Cyril continued to argue frequently. While Ruby was pregnant with their second child, she took baby Vivian and left Cyril for the last time.

On November 9, 1922, Ruby gave birth to another daughter and named her Dorothy Jean. Family and friends often called the little girl "Dottie." Throughout her childhood, Dorothy never saw her father. Ruby told Dorothy and Vivian their father wanted nothing to do with his daughters, but this was not true. Cyril searched for his family. When he finally found them, he begged Ruby to come home, but she refused.

Cyril finally filed for divorce and demanded to have custody of Dorothy and Vivian. He did not think Ruby would care for his daughters properly. Ruby hired lawyers, and Cyril did not fight Ruby for custody. Still, the divorce proceedings dragged on for many

Too Cute for Her Own Good

Dorothy was a sensitive and sweet little girl. She was also very pretty. Adults often took notice of her. A playmate, another girl named Dorothy—Dorothy Hughes McConnell—grew tired of hearing adults praising Dorothy's beauty. McConnell said, "I can remember this girl that was so cute with this pretty hair, and whenever she got all these compliments, I'd beat her up."[1]

years. Ruby wanted Cyril out of
her life and kept him out of her
daughters' lives for many years.
For some reason, Ruby wanted
her daughters to think Cyril had
abandoned his family. For many
years, Ruby even told the girls he was
dead. Dorothy grew up believing her
father did not love her or want her.

DREAMS OF FAME

Meanwhile, Ruby was busy making
a new life for herself. She worked
as a maid, but she dreamed of
performing on stage. Ruby sang and
recited poetry at church functions,
practicing at home in front of Vivian
and Dorothy. One night, Ruby

Fatherless Christmas

One Christmas Eve night
when Dorothy was small,
Ruby woke Vivian and
Dorothy and told them to
hide in the attic because
Santa was near. In real-
ity, Cyril had come to
the house. He wanted to
take his daughters home
with him for Christmas,
but Ruby refused. Doro-
thy and Vivian heard their
mother yelling and real-
ized it was their father, not
Santa. They began crying
and were very frightened.
Then, the door slammed
and Cyril left. In later
years, Dorothy despised
her father's emotional
weakness and wished he
had been stronger and not
given up so easily.

came home from work and said she was too tired to
perform at church that night. She was supposed to
recite the poem "In the Morning" by her favorite
African-American poet, Paul Laurence Dunbar.

"I'll do it for you, Mama," said Dorothy, who
was only three years old.[2] Ruby was amused at first,
but when Dorothy recited the entire poem perfectly,

mimicking her mother's dramatic way of rehearsing it, Ruby was amazed. She could not wait to show off her little girl's talent, so Dorothy performed the Dunbar poem at church that night. Little Dorothy was a big hit.

Soon, Ruby was training Dorothy to sing, dance, and do gymnastic routines. Vivian wanted to be a part of the act, too, so Ruby taught both girls to perform. She often told her daughters she did not want them to become maids or servants. She wanted them to have a better life than she had.

Paul Laurence Dunbar

Paul Laurence Dunbar (1872–1906) was the first African-American poet to become popular among both black and white audiences. His poetry was well known in the late nineteenth and early twentieth centuries. Much of his work dealt with the inequality and poverty African Americans faced. Dunbar often wrote dialect poetry: poems with a specific style of speaking to reflect the person in the poem. "In the Morning," which Dorothy recited for her first performance, is a dialect poem about a mother trying to get her son out of bed:

'LIAS! 'Lias! Bless de Lawd!
Don'you know de day's erbroad?
Ef you don' git up, you scamp,
Dey'll be trouble in dis camp. . . .

Ma'ch yo'se'f an wash yo' face,
Don' you splattah all de place;
I got somep'n else to do,
'Sides jes' cleanin' aftah you. . . .

Fol' yo' han's an' bow yo' haid—
Wait ontwell de blessin's said;
"Lawd, have mussy on ouah souls—"
(Don'you daih to tech dem rolls—)
"Bless de food we gwine to eat—"
(You set still—I see yo' feet;
You jes' try dat trick agin!)
"Gin us peace an' joy. Amen!"[3]

A New Ma-Ma

Around 1926, Ruby met a woman named Geneva Williams, a music teacher. Ruby and Williams developed a romantic relationship, and Williams moved in with Ruby and the girls. While Ruby worked as a maid to earn money and pay bills, Williams took over caring for the house and training the girls. This was very confusing to Vivian and Dorothy, who were told to call this stranger "Auntie Ma-Ma."

Auntie Ma-Ma was strict and demanding. She expected the girls to do chores perfectly, to behave properly, and to obey promptly. When the girls made mistakes, Auntie Ma-Ma became furious and punished them. She had a terrible temper and frequently slapped the girls across the face and on the arms or legs or spanked them hard with a hairbrush. Many times, the girls did not know what they had done to make Auntie Ma-Ma so angry. Unfortunately, their mother never defended them. She allowed Williams to abuse the girls.

Auntie Ma-Ma trained the girls in music. She not only wanted the girls to perform perfectly at home, but she also wanted them to perform perfectly on stage. Auntie Ma-Ma drilled the girls in singing,

Ruby Dandridge, Dorothy's mother, was also an actress.

dancing, and acting. She pushed them hard every day and even at night. When Dorothy and Vivian were old enough to attend school, Auntie Ma-Ma decided to teach them at home, so she would have more time to make them practice. Vivian and Dorothy were seldom allowed to play with friends because it interfered with their rehearsals. Although they performed beautifully, Auntie Ma-Ma always criticized them. She demanded perfection, and Dorothy grew up feeling her best was never good enough.

The Wonder Children

Auntie Ma-Ma was critical of Vivian and Dorothy, but black audiences thought the little Dandridge girls were terrific. Dorothy and Vivian were called the Wonder Children because they did amazing acrobatic stunts in addition to singing, dancing, and reciting. The Wonder Children performed in black churches and schools all over the South, traveling from their Ohio home to earn a living. Ruby quit working as a maid and took over managing the Wonder Children's publicity, planning the shows with Auntie Ma-Ma. The Wonder Children earned several hundred dollars a month, which was a very good income in the late 1920s.

Life on the road was difficult on Dorothy. She was often exhausted from traveling and performing, and she was not used to the extreme heat in the

South. She also faced segregation. In addition, Auntie Ma-Ma would not allow the girls to have any fun exploring the towns they visited because she thought doing so was foolish. She wanted the girls to stay disciplined and to save their energy for the stage.

Dorothy was deprived of her father, neglected by her mother, and raised by a woman who abused her. To cope, she retreated from reality and spent many hours in a fantasy world, where she could disappear from everyone. Once outgoing and daring, Dorothy became solitary and shy, except when she was on stage.

First Tastes of Racism

While traveling in the South during the years of the Wonder Children, Dorothy learned about segregation. She saw signs indicating that public places everywhere, including restaurants, restrooms, theaters, and sections on buses and trains, were for white people only. "For Coloreds" signs marked areas where she was allowed to go, but she had to stay away from areas designated by signs "For Whites." Ruby and Auntie Ma-Ma also told Dorothy to behave respectfully around white people in the South so she would not get in trouble.

The only time she felt loved was when audiences responded to her performances—or afterward, when her mother would kiss, hug, and praise her for doing a good job. Only on stage was Dorothy allowed to act like a joyful, free, and playful child. While her difficult childhood caused young Dorothy much anxiety, it also prepared her for challenges that life would bring—especially in show business.

Dorothy faced segregation, such as separate drinking fountains for blacks, while traveling as part of the Wonder Children.

After the stock market crashed, Dorothy's family moved to Los Angeles, California. Hollywood and Vine was a popular LA spot at the time.

CALIFORNIA GIRL

Dorothy was seven years old when the US stock market crashed in 1929. This event was one of the causes of the Great Depression, a time of economic crisis that affected the United States and the world. During this time, millions of

Americans, including the Wonder Children, were
out of work. Ruby looked for work as a maid, but few
jobs were available. Like so many families during the
Depression, Dorothy's family grew poor and often
did not have enough to eat.

Yet somehow, Ruby managed to save enough
money to buy four bus tickets to Los Angeles,
California. Ruby was certain that she, Auntie
Ma-Ma, Vivian, and Dorothy could make a living
there. Los Angeles was home to Hollywood, a perfect
place for the Wonder Children.

Although Auntie Ma-Ma finally enrolled
Dorothy and Vivian in public school when they were
eight and nine years old, she still did not allow them
freedom to play like normal children. Every day after
school and all day Saturday, the girls had to attend
dancing and singing classes.

Vivian did well in school, but Dorothy struggled.
Growing up touring had been hard on her, and
she could barely read. Whenever Dorothy had to
learn something, she got others to read to her, and
she memorized the information. Teachers allowed
Dorothy to pass classes because she was charming and
intelligent, even though she could not read.

Three Dandridge Sisters

At singing and dancing school, Dorothy and Vivian befriended a girl named Etta Jones. The three girls rehearsed their songs together and their voices blended very well, so Ruby began scheming to make money with the talented girls. She decided to make Dorothy, Vivian, and Etta into a singing and dancing trio called the Dandridge Sisters. Now, the girls had to practice even more.

The Dandridge Sisters found work performing in local theaters and singing with other groups. Then, in 1934, when Dorothy was 12, the Dandridge Sisters entered a Los Angeles radio contest. They were the only African Americans to enter and were quite surprised when they came in first place. Winning this contest drew attention to the Dandridge Sisters and helped them get better work. They made small appearances in movies and performed with a circus in Hawaii for a few months.

Not a Real Sister

Although the Dandridge Sisters seemed like family on stage, Dorothy resented Etta's being promoted as her sister. Vivian was her only sister. Dorothy shared things with Vivian she never shared with anyone else, including how she felt about Etta.

Etta did not like Dorothy very much, either. According to Etta, Dorothy was overly emotional and erratic. She explained, "The two of us weren't friendly, . . . but we never fought and argued."[1] Audiences did not know about the friction. On stage, the three girls were the perfect image of unity, dressed in matching outfits, dancing in unison, and singing in beautiful harmony.

In 1937, the Dandridge Sisters were chosen to appear in the Groucho Marx film *A Day at the Races*, now considered a classic comedy. The following year, they appeared in the film *Going Places* with Louis Armstrong. But 1938 brought an even greater opportunity: The Dandridge Sisters got their big break when they were booked to perform at the famous Cotton Club in Harlem, an area of New York City.

THE COTTON CLUB

The Cotton Club was a unique nightclub that featured the most talented black entertainers of the day. Ethel Waters, Cab Calloway, Duke Ellington, and Lena Horne all became famous after performing at the Cotton Club. Ruby knew the Dandridge Sisters could not pass up an opportunity to perform there.

During the girls' first day in New York, Auntie Ma-Ma took them shopping for dresses that would make them look less like teenagers and more like sophisticated women. When they arrived at the Cotton Club, Dorothy met the dancing duo the Nicholas Brothers. The younger brother, Harold, could not take his eyes off Dorothy. The 15-year-old was growing into a stunning beauty. Worried that men would try to take advantage of the girls, Auntie Ma-Ma announced at the club, "Do not come near these girls. They are flirtatious. They are silly. They are virgins."[2] If any man bothered the girls, she threatened to have him arrested.

Even so, Harold and Dorothy quickly became friends. Auntie Ma-Ma realized that having such a successful performer as a friend might help advance the girls' careers. She allowed Harold

The Cotton Club

During the Prohibition Era (1920–1933), it was illegal to sell, transport, and consume alcohol in the United States. To get around the law, some gangsters opened an exclusive nightclub called the Cotton Club in the middle of Harlem, New York's prosperous black neighborhood. The Cotton Club soon became the hottest place around and grew famous for featuring the very best African-American entertainers. Only high-society white people could attend the show, and only top-notch black performers could be in the show. In *Tap: The Greatest Tap Dance Stars and Their Stories, 1900–1955,* Richard Frank describes the club: "If you were white, it was the place to go. If you were black, it was the show to be in."[3]

Until Prohibition ended, people could be arrested for being any place that served alcohol, so audiences and performers alike were taking a big risk simply by being at the Cotton Club. But it was worth it. For audiences, a night at the Cotton Club meant seeing one exciting, exotic act after another. For performers, having a gig at the Cotton Club meant being seen by some of the most well-connected people in show business.

The famous Cotton Club closed in 1940 due to financial difficulties. The Dandridge Sisters were on tour in Europe at the time—an opportunity they probably would not have had without the Cotton Club.

to see Dorothy but only if they were chaperoned. She never let them be alone together.

Auntie Ma-Ma also limited the teens' fun. Their schedule was filled with rehearsals, and they performed three shows a night: the first show was at 7:00 p.m., the second was at 10:00 p.m., and the third show was around 2:00 a.m.

The Dandridge Sisters' Cotton Club debut was on September 28, 1938. They had such a successful first run that they were asked to return for another season the following fall. The trio played until spring 1940. Critics wrote favorable reviews of their act, which were published in newspapers across the United States.

TOUR IN EUROPE

The teenagers had other exciting projects. In June 1939, between engagements at the Cotton Club, the Dandridge Sisters boarded the

The Famous Nicholas Brothers

Dorothy and Vivian were not the only black youngsters making a living as entertainers. Fayard and Harold Nicholas grew up in show business performing as the Nicholas Brothers. They began tap dancing professionally in 1930, when Fayard was 11 and Harold was seven. The duo amazed audiences with their moves, which were as smooth, polished, and sophisticated as any adult dancer's. The two boys put their own creative spin on tap dancing, including flips, splits, and acrobatic stunts. Audiences loved them. Superstar dancer Fred Astaire was a big fan. When Harold and Fayard met Astaire and had their photo taken with him, Astaire said, "At last I'm with the brothers!"[4]

One of Dandridge's first movies was Going Places *with Louis Armstrong.*

Queen Mary luxury ocean liner in New York and set sail for Europe while Ruby remained in Los Angeles. The trio performed at the Palladium in London, England, and at various theaters throughout England, Scotland, and Ireland. British audiences

loved the trio just as much as
Americans did.

Unfortunately, the Dandridge
Sisters' European performances
were interrupted by World War II
(1939–1945). When the girls arrived
in London, Germany had already
invaded Czechoslovakia, and Italy
had taken over Albania. Then, in
September 1939, Great Britain and
France declared war on Germany,
which began bombing Great Britain.
The Dandridge Sisters were terrified
and wondered if they would survive.
Finally, they booked passage on a
ship and returned safely to the
United States.

DOROTHY STRIKES BACK

The Dandridge Sisters' success
did not end the abuse by Auntie
Ma-Ma. Even though Dorothy was
nearly 17, Auntie Ma-Ma kept hitting
her. When a friend of Dorothy's got
pregnant, Auntie Ma-Ma worried the

Unexpected Reunion

Cyril Dandridge had lost
hope of seeing his daugh-
ters again until he read
an article about them
performing at the Cotton
Club. He traveled to New
York and arranged to see
Dorothy and Vivian, who
were shocked to learn
Ruby had lied to them
about their father. Cyril
tried to get to know the
girls, but the situation was
awkward and confusing
for Dorothy. Although she
had longed for her father
all her life, she would not
give him another chance.
Vivian, however, did stay
in touch with Cyril and
visited him in later years.

same thing would happen to Dorothy. One night, Auntie Ma-Ma forcefully held down Dorothy on the bed while she tried to examine her. Dorothy struggled hard and then slapped Auntie Ma-Ma in the face. Auntie Ma-Ma hit back. Dorothy furiously kept hitting as hard as she could.

Dorothy had never struck anyone before, but it felt good to fight back. Auntie Ma-Ma finally gave up, and Dorothy burst out crying and left the room—exhausted but victorious. This was the last time Auntie Ma-Ma hit Dorothy. Even so, Auntie Ma-Ma's cruel influence continued, and Dorothy began planning ways to get free from her forever.

In 1939, the Dandridge Sisters sailed from New York to Europe on the luxury liner Queen Mary.

Fayard Nicholas, left, and Harold Nicholas, Dorothy's first husband were a wildly popular dancing team.

MRS. NICHOLAS

y the time the Dandridge Sisters returned from Europe in autumn 1939, Dorothy had decided to go solo, and she did just that in 1940. At 18, she was tired of being a Dandridge Sister and tired of Auntie Ma-Ma having control over her. She auditioned for a role in a Los Angeles theater production of *Meet the People* and won the part. *Meet the People* was an all-white production, and her role was intended for a white actress. But Dorothy was certain she could play any part—and she was right. Critics and audiences loved her, especially Harold Nicholas.

Dorothy and Harold were now dating steadily and in love. Dorothy admired him for his talent and his confidence. Having been disappointed in her father's weak, passive personality, Dorothy was drawn to men with powerful egos. As her best friend once said, "Dottie didn't like wimps."[1]

Working in show business often kept the couple apart. While the Nicholas Brothers were on tour in one part of the United States, Dorothy was somewhere else filming a movie or singing with one of several orchestras. This separation stirred

Soundies

Performers in the 1940s often found short gigs making soundies, which were similar to music videos. People watched these short films on a refrigerator-sized, coin-operated machine called a Panoram. For a dime, a person could watch a three-minute song-and-dance or comedy routine on a small screen.

Many soundies perpetuated racist stereotypes by portraying African Americans as simple-minded, superstitious, and carefree. Nonetheless, the performers were highly talented. Some of Dorothy's soundies—such as *Cow Cow Boogie*, *Zoot Suit*, and *Lazybones*—can be seen online at YouTube.

feelings of insecurity in Dorothy, and she often cried when Harold did not stay in touch with her.

When the Nicholas Brothers came back to Los Angeles, they asked Dorothy to join them in a song-and-dance number for the film *Sun Valley Serenade* (1941). Dorothy was thrilled. The trio performed to the song "Chattanooga Choo Choo," helping it become a huge pop hit.

In 1941, job offers seemed to flood Dorothy's way. Harold wanted Dorothy to marry him, but she wanted to wait and focus on her blossoming career. She won parts in the films *Sundown* and *Bahama Passage*, but her biggest break of the year was the lead in *Jump for Joy*, a stage musical with an all-black cast of prominent actors.

A Fairy-Tale Wedding

Established as a successful solo performer, Dandridge finally agreed to marry Nicholas. The couple wed on September 6, 1942. Radiant in a white dress, Dandridge was full of romantic hopes and dreams for married life. She and Nicholas moved into a little house in a nice neighborhood. Finally free from Auntie Ma-Ma, Dandridge threw all her energy into creating a lovely home. She

Dandridge joined the Nicholas Brothers for the song-and-dance number "Chattanooga Choo Choo" in the film Sun Valley Serenade.

redecorated the house, kept it spotlessly clean, and cooked delicious meals for her husband. More than anything, she longed to be loved and cherished.

But Dandridge's storybook notions of romantic marriage were soon disappointed. Her husband seldom stayed home or spent time with her. When he was not performing, he was on the golf course or with his friends. Dandridge was also certain he was seeing other women. The couple began to argue almost every day.

Jump for Joy

Jump for Joy was an all-black musical that showcased African-American wit and intelligence by poking fun at racial stereotypes, such as Uncle Tom. The term *Uncle Tom*, popularized from the 1851 novel *Uncle Tom's Cabin* by Harriet Beecher Stowe, is used to describe a black person who tries to please white people by being subservient to them.

"In *Jump for Joy*, Uncle Tom is dead," wrote the *Los Angeles Tribune*, and everyone sings songs of freedom.[2] Duke Ellington, whose band played throughout the musical, said the play gave black audiences pride: "The Negroes always left proudly, with their chests sticking out."[3] *Jump for Joy* attracted a wide audience, from average folks to leading intellectuals such as Langston Hughes to famous Hollywood celebrities.

Dandridge was proud to be part of this production, and she did well. But her performance was not as good as it might have been because she was working on two projects at once. She performed in *Jump for Joy* every night, arrived home well after midnight, and got up at 5:00 every morning to film *Bahama Passage*. She only got three to four hours of sleep each night, so she was too exhausted to give her best performance.

FINDING A BEST FRIEND

One night when Dandridge and Nicholas were out, their car was hit by a drunk driver. Nicholas was unhurt, but Dandridge was thrown from the car and then hospitalized with a back injury. While she languished in the hospital, Nicholas played golf. Dandridge was all alone until her sister-in-law, Fayard's wife Geri

Pate Nicholas, visited the hospital. Geri visited Dandridge every day. By the time Dandridge was released from the hospital, the two women had become best friends.

Geri was well educated and intelligent. Her knowledge of politics and literature fired Dandridge's own intellectual curiosity. With Geri's encouragement, Dandridge developed her reading skills. One of Dandridge's favorite subjects was psychology, and reading about it helped her understand herself and her family.

BECOMING A MOTHER

In winter 1943, Dandridge was thrilled to find out she was pregnant. She believed that being a father would change her husband's self-centered patterns, but it did not. Nicholas continued spending his free time with his friends, and Dandridge continued arguing with him about his alienation.

On September 1, 1943, Dandridge woke up in pain. Although she was sure she was in labor, Nicholas told her not to worry. He took Dandridge to Geri's house for the day, saying he would come back later—they figured he went golfing.

Dandridge and Nicholas with family and friends on their wedding day

But Dandridge was indeed in labor. She refused
to let anyone but her husband take her to the
hospital, but no one could find Nicholas. Geri
finally convinced her to go to the hospital, but the
baby was already on the way. After a difficult birth,
Dandridge delivered a beautiful baby girl. She
named her daughter Harolyn Suzanne, and the
child's nickname was Lynn.

Dandridge was soon optimistic again, dreaming
rosy fantasies about having a perfect little family.

Motherhood came naturally to her, and she loved taking care of her little girl. Soon after Lynn's birth, Geri had a baby boy named Tony. The two young mothers spent a lot of time together with their children, taking walks and playing in the park.

TROUBLE AND SORROW

As Lynn grew older, Dandridge began to fear something was wrong with her child. Lynn did not seem to be developing normally, and she did not talk. She was not learning, and most disturbing of all, she did not recognize her own mother. Dandridge took Lynn to specialists and read every book she could find, but no one could tell her how to help Lynn. Nicholas spent even more time away to avoid the sad situation at home, which only added to Dandridge's sorrow.

Lynn had to be watched constantly. She was uncontrollable and barely slept. Being on constant

Lynn's Difficult Birth

In the 1940s, people used the word *retarded* to describe various problems with mental development. Dandridge was told her daughter, Lynn, was severely retarded due to oxygen deprivation during birth. Lynn's brain damage was irreversible, and there was no hope of improvement. Dandridge was devastated to find out she would never hear her beloved child call her mama. Overcome by guilt, Dandridge believed she was to blame for Lynn's condition, although her doctor said it was not her fault. Dandridge thought if she had gone to the hospital sooner, Lynn would have been fine.

guard and worrying about her daughter took a heavy toll on Dandridge's mental health. She became depressed and often could not leave the house.

When Dandridge's doctor advised her to let someone else care for the child, she enlisted the help of a woman named Jonesy, who was in her seventies. When Jonesy became ill and could no longer care for Lynn, Dandridge tried to find another nanny, but no one could handle Lynn. Finally, Ruby and Auntie Ma-Ma offered to take Lynn if Dandridge would pay them. Dandridge agreed. Many people could not understand how Dandridge could turn her daughter over to the very woman who had abused her, but Dandridge was desperate. Her marriage was a failure, her daughter was untreatable, and all her hopes and dreams had been shattered—except for her dream of being a movie star. ⌐

Jump for Joy *poked fun at racial stereotypes such as* Uncle Tom *from the Harriet Beecher Stowe book* Uncle Tom's Cabin.

Dandridge was good friends with fellow actress Marilyn Monroe.

STARTING OVER

andridge's dreams of having a happy family were over. Heartbroken, she slipped into a deep depression. She overdosed on sleeping pills and had to be rushed to the hospital to have her stomach pumped.

Dandridge pressed on with a new determination to live her life. In 1949, she told Nicholas she wanted to return to her career—and she wanted a divorce. She left Nicholas. She also enrolled in the Actor's Lab in Hollywood, where many serious actors studied. In classes at the lab, Dandridge met a young actress named Marilyn Monroe, and the two women became good friends.

A New Act

Around this time, Dandridge also met Phil Moore, a famous composer, pianist, and music coach. Moore knew Dandridge would appeal to black and white audiences alike, so he began coaching her. He also coached Monroe and Ava Gardner. Dandridge made friends with both women, and the three beauties often attended parties together. But of all the beautiful women Moore worked with, none of them captured his heart like Dandridge. He arranged songs for her and helped her choose the

International Beauty

Dandridge was known for her beauty—her skin color in particular. Best friend Geri described it as "pure café-au-lait."[1] One writer was especially taken by her coloring. Dandridge described an encounter with a screen-writer who grabbed her and said, "Your skin is neuter. Your skin is all the skin colorings of the world. It is chameleon; it changes in each swath of light, ranging from white to dark by the instant. It is East Indian soft, it is South American blend, it can be Israeli, Gypsy, Egyptian, Latin. What is your color? It is a blend of the world's skin tones."[2]

perfect gowns for a solo act. Working together, they created an image of a classy, sexy songstress.

Although Moore had prepared Dandridge well for her solo nightclub act, she was terrified of performing. One night, her intense anxiety and stage fright caused her to hyperventilate, and she had to go to the hospital, where she was given oxygen. Moore helped her through these rough times, reminding her how talented she was and that audiences loved her. As her confidence returned, she delivered wonderful performances.

In 1949, Dandridge was the headline act at a supper club in Las Vegas, Nevada, called the Bingo. Because of racism, Dandridge was not allowed to stay in the city, so she had to find a room on the outskirts of Las Vegas. Also, at the Bingo, she was not allowed to use the front door, to speak to the guests, or to eat in the dining room. Instead of a dressing room, she was given an old, cluttered storage room in which to change and eat her meals.

Despite being discriminated against in Las Vegas, Dandridge wowed the crowds. Critics published great reviews of her act. Her reputation as a fabulous nightclub performer grew, which attracted the attention of movie producers and directors.

MORE MOVIES

The year 1950 brought a new decade to the world and personal and professional changes to Dandridge. On September 29, a judge in Los Angeles made an initial divorce judgment. In October 1951, a final judgment was made and she was legally divorced from Nicholas. She also got a new film project in 1951, when she won the role of Queen Melmendi in the movie *Tarzan's Peril*. And she was featured on the cover of *Ebony* magazine's April issue, in which she was proclaimed "Hollywood's New Glamour Queen."[3]

Also in 1951, Dandridge appeared in *The Harlem Globetrotters*. The film was memorable because

The Mixed Dancing Scandal

In summer 1948, the students at the Actor's Lab held a street fair to raise money. There were food booths, skits, live music, and dancing. At one point, white actor Anthony Quinn danced with Dandridge. Soon, other acting students of different races were dancing together and having a wonderful time. Some people were offended and angry to see white people dancing with black people.

Two local newspapers ran articles saying such activity was anti-American and could lead to race riots and even the destruction of the United States. Dandridge and the other actors at the lab were outraged. The articles did not mention Dandridge's name, but she felt she had to respond to the accusations. She wrote a letter to the *California Eagle* newspaper that showed the hypocrisy of accusing the Actor's Lab of being undemocratic, when "students are selected on the basis of ability, rather than on the color of their skin."[4]

it portrayed a young African-American couple in love, which was uncommon. Moviegoers were accustomed to films portraying African Americans as servants or buffoons. Once again, Dandridge received wonderful reviews.

LYNN'S NEW HOME

While Dandridge worked on her career and her life as a single woman, Lynn was being raised by Ruby and Auntie Ma-Ma. By the time Lynn was seven years old, the two women could not manage her. Vivian tried to help, but it was clear that Lynn needed to be cared for by a professional. At the time, there were schools for children like Lynn, but they were only for white children.

Dandridge refused to put Lynn in an institution. She explained,

> I thought of an institution as a place with a lot of beds and where they . . . throw you around like animals. I just couldn't see her there.[5]

Finally, Dandridge found someone to care for her daughter. Helen Calhoun cared for such children in her own home. Lynn stayed with Calhoun for 13 years.

Racism, Hollywood Style

Dandridge grew increasingly frustrated when white actresses were cast as ethnic or mixed-race characters, robbing black actresses of excellent roles. Hollywood was afraid audiences were not ready for a nonwhite leading lady in a romantic situation with a white actor. At the time, interracial relationships were unacceptable to most Americans, so Hollywood played it safe.

Faced with the challenge of finding work in Hollywood as a black actress, Dandridge often returned to singing in nightclubs to earn a living. She referred to the nightclubs where she sang as "saloons," a term intended to reflect their undesirable quality. The people who went to these clubs were not sophisticated or respectable. Instead, they were usually men who drank and smoked excessively and often treated her disrespectfully.

Communist Paranoia

During the 1950s and 1960s, anyone who worked for change in society could be called a commie, a pinko, or another negative term for someone who supports communism. Communism was a radical political idea, and racial equality was a radical social idea. Many African Americans who worked for racial equality were considered radicals and suspected of being Communists, even though they had no ties to communism. The media helped spread the panic and paranoia, which significantly slowed the progress of racial equality in the United States.

Dandridge did not like this work and often became so nervous before a show that she would vomit. But she did it to further her career and to pay for Lynn's care. With Moore as her pianist, she made a whirl of appearances during the 1950s in the most elite clubs in the United States and Europe. Audiences loved her, reviewers raved about her, and other performers were impressed. And Dandridge's saloon singing soon brought her more of the work she truly loved—acting.

Wearing black velvet, Dandridge performed at La Vie En Rose in New York City in 1952.

Dandridge in 1953

A Rising Star

Dandridge's relationship with Moore benefited her professionally and personally. Moore helped her create a successful singing career. He was also in love with her. However, he was extremely controlling. While he wanted her to be successful, he also seemed to take all the credit for her success. Rather than encourage Dandridge to trust her instincts, Moore often criticized her ideas to keep her dependent on his judgment.

As Dandridge's confidence grew, she tired of Moore's possessiveness. Soon, she found a new agent—Earl Mills—who would become a loyal friend.

BRIGHT ROAD

In 1952, Mills helped Dandridge land an important role in a new movie called *Bright Road*, opposite Harry Belafonte. Dandridge's role was that of Jane Richards, a new schoolteacher trying to help her students, especially one troubled boy named C. J.

While Dandridge enjoyed working closely with the young African-American actors playing her students, she sometimes found it troubling.

Dating on the Set

Dandridge was divorced when she began filming *Bright Road*, so she was free to date again. She flirted with her costar, Harry Belafonte, and the two began an on-again, off-again romance that lasted a few years. Dandridge also had a romantic relationship with the film's director, Gerald Mayer. Mayer was white, and interracial romances were frowned upon by much of US society at that time. The couple eventually split.

These nine-year-olds were the same age as her
daughter, but Lynn would never sit in a classroom or
talk, read, and learn like them. Dandridge often had
to choke back tears of sorrow for her daughter.

Bright Road was released in theaters in 1953, and it
earned good reviews. *Ebony* magazine featured a full
article on the film and put Dandridge's photograph
on the cover of the April 1953 issue.

NIGHTCLUB GODDESS

After *Bright Road*, Mills scheduled a busy nightclub
tour for Dandridge, now 30 years old. He also made
certain she received the great publicity she deserved.
By this time, Dandridge was a famous nightclub
performer, and people flocked to see her. Both *Life*
and *Variety* magazines published her touring schedule,
complete with glamorous color photos. Dandridge
had a personal assistant to take care of her wardrobe
and make sure she was comfortable. Her assistant
also kept away annoying male fans.

Now that Dandridge had earned the status of a
"golden goddess headliner," she was more intolerant
than ever of racial prejudice.[1] Nowhere was this
bigotry more upsetting to her than in Las Vegas. In
1953, Mills booked Dandridge for two weeks at the

city's prestigious Last Frontier Hotel. The hotel management agreed to let her stay in one of its luxury suites but only after Mills insisted. However, Dandridge was told not to go near the swimming pool. If she did, the pool would be drained.

Dandridge was outraged. As described by biographer Donald Bogle,

> *She would storm through her suite, lashing out her anger and her despair. Here she was in the land of the free and the home of the brave—and she couldn't use a swimming pool.*[2]

If Dandridge even hinted that she wanted to swim, the hotel would close the pool and put up a sign saying it was closed for maintenance. On one occasion, Dandridge and her friends were shocked to see the pool empty and dry. The hotel's management had drained the pool just to keep her out.

Peter Lawford

Dandridge dated British-born actor Peter Lawford during the 1950s. She was smitten by his dreamy good looks, gentle manners, and English accent. The two became quite close but could never marry or even openly date. In some US states, it was a crime for blacks and whites to marry. Some people were even imprisoned for interracial marriage in Alabama. Lawford told Dandridge, "Look, I love you. . . . I would like to marry you. But let's face it, . . . I wouldn't work another day if we married. And neither would you."[3] Dandridge's dreams of romance were crushed again.

Always the professional, Dandridge did not let her resentment affect her work. Of her performances at the Last Frontier, *Variety* magazine wrote, "Miss Dandridge has skyrocketed into that strata of rare mesmerizers. She looks gorgeous, wears stunning gowns, has a bewitching sexiness."[4] The *Las Vegas Review-Journal* reported that "she is pelted with roars from the audience of 'bravo! bravo!—more! more!'. . . Dorothy has taken another long step up the stairway to the stars."[5]

The Climb

That stairway to the stars was long and difficult, and Dandridge still had more steps to climb. She continued to be confronted with racism. In St. Louis, Missouri, she stayed at the Chase Hotel, where she was scheduled to perform in the hotel's dining room. She was the first black performer booked by the hotel, which

Poor Auntie Ma-Ma

During the early 1950s, Dandridge's mother, Ruby, broke up with Geneva Williams (Auntie Ma-Ma) and began living with a new woman. In desperation, Williams begged Dandridge's best friend, Geri, to speak to Dandridge about helping her or giving her some money. When Dandridge heard about this, she flatly refused. "Look, I've been in therapy all these years to try to work out my problems," Dandridge told Geri. "I do not want to be bothered with that woman. Keep her away from me."[6]

did not allow African Americans to use the front door. Dandridge agreed to perform if the hotel opened its doors to African Americans and allowed them to make dinner reservations to watch her show.

In 1953, Hollywood buzzed with news of a new musical film that would feature an all-black cast: *Carmen Jones*. It was to be an adaptation of Georges Bizet's celebrated opera *Carmen* and directed by well-known studio executive Otto Preminger. The film offered the opportunity of a lifetime to African-American actors.

Otto the Terrible

Otto Preminger was born in Austria in 1905 to Jewish parents. He came to the United States in 1935 to escape Nazi persecution. He was both a director and an actor and worked on stage and in films. Ironically, he often played brutal Nazi characters on stage and in movies, such as *Stalag 17* (1953).

Preminger had a reputation for behaving badly. Journalist Geoffrey MacNab wrote this unflattering description of Preminger:

> When he was displeased, his eyes would bulge, his cheeks swell, his veins pop, his face turn puce, and you could imagine that steam was about to come out of his ears and nostrils. . . . Some actors at the receiving end of one of his tirades claim never to have recovered from the experience."[7]

Such behavior earned him the nicknames Otto the Terrible and Otto the Ogre.

By the mid-1960s, Preminger's directing career was fading, but he continued to act. In 1966, he made a guest appearance on the television series *Batman* as the villain Mr. Freeze. He had asked to play a part. As with other projects, he was rude and difficult to work with. Preminger died from lung cancer and Alzheimer's disease in 1986. He was 80.

Dandridge's increasing success and popularity seemed to make her a natural choice for at least an audition, but Preminger saw Dandridge as sophisticated and an entertainer, not the fiery main character, Carmen Jones.

Becoming Carmen

Mills had an office across the hall from Otto Preminger's brother, Ingo Preminger. Mills practically begged Ingo to get Dandridge a meeting with his powerful brother. In the end, Otto granted Dandridge a meeting, but he still did not intend to let her audition for the role of Carmen.

Mills accompanied Dandridge to meet the distinguished director. Dandridge, 31, dressed in a modest outfit, pulled her hair back in a ponytail, and wore little makeup. When Preminger began talking about the role of Carmen, he insisted that Dandridge was not earthy enough for the part. According to Dandridge, Preminger said, "I seemed too sweet, too regal, that he didn't think I'd do."[8] He would, however, allow her to audition for the part of Cindy Lou, the sweet, jilted girlfriend. Mills took a script and thanked Preminger, but he and Dandridge later schemed about how she could

A poster for the movie Carmen Jones *was featured in a traveling exhibition that covered 80 years in African-American filmmaking history.*

audition as Carmen. Dandridge had no intention of playing Cindy Lou.

That evening, Dandridge told her sister, Vivian, how angry she was that Preminger had not let her audition for the role of Carmen. Vivian said it was because she had dressed for the meeting as if she

Proud of Her Roots

The success Dandridge experienced threatened to take her far from her roots. At the height of her career, she moved in a world of powerful white people that included very few blacks. Best friend Geri, concerned that Dandridge might lose touch with who she was, helped her stay grounded. "I just could not let the White community absorb her life," explained Geri, who often took Dandridge to events sponsored by the Urban League, a nonprofit organization dedicated to empowering African Americans. Dandridge also spoke at some of these functions. "Dottie took pride in it, too," said Geri.[10] Dandridge also became a lifetime member of the NAACP.

were going to church. Vivian told her to dress and to act like Carmen the next time she saw Preminger. Mills agreed. Even Ruby helped Dandridge envision how Carmen might behave. Ruby showed Dandridge how to walk more provocatively, swinging her hips, wagging her head, and looking people up and down.

On the day Dandridge auditioned for the part of Cindy Lou, she wore a black wig that looked tousled and wild, a skirt with a slit up the leg, a low-cut peasant blouse, and dark, sensuous makeup. She sashayed into Preminger's office swinging her hips and looking nothing like the sweet Cindy Lou. Preminger was completely surprised and exclaimed, "My God. It's Carmen!"[9]

Dandridge posed in a pink brocade dress that she later wore to perform the song "Talk Sweet to Me" during her nightclub performances.

Dandridge attends a press reception at the Savoy Hotel in London in 1956.

THE FIRST AFRICAN-AMERICAN MOVIE STAR

reminger was so impressed with how Dandridge captured the image of Carmen Jones that he arranged for her to do a screen test for the part. Two other actresses were also auditioning for the role: Joyce Bryant and Elizabeth

Foster. Dandridge would have to outshine them both—and she did. When Preminger viewed her screen test, he said, "It's the best screen test I've ever seen."[1]

Soon after Dandridge won the part of Carmen, she had a major anxiety attack and would not leave her apartment. She said she did not want to do the movie. She may have been afraid of Preminger, who had a reputation for bullying actors. She was also worried the African-American community would object to the film because Carmen's character was a negative portrayal of an African-American woman.

After refusing to leave the house for several days, Dandridge received a visit from Preminger. He spoke gently with her, assuring her he would be supportive on the set. He built up her confidence and told her making *Carmen Jones* "would firmly establish her as a major motion

Role Model

Many young actresses on the set of *Carmen Jones* looked up to Dandridge. Olga James, who played Cindy Lou, said of the leading lady, "She behaved like a star. . . . She was simple, . . . elegant, . . . well-mannered, . . . disciplined. She was focused on the work."[2] Diahann Carroll made her film debut in *Carmen Jones*. According to Carroll, Dandridge seemed "concerned only with improving her performance. So much was riding on it that she seemed to be living in a constant state of anxiety."[3] Carroll found herself wanting to comfort and protect Dandridge.

picture actress."[4] Preminger wanted his Carmen to succeed—and he was falling in love with her.

PLAYING CARMEN

During filming, Dandridge was intensely focused. While other actors relaxed, joked around, and ate meals together to unwind during breaks, Dandridge retired to her dressing room alone to study and rehearse her part.

If some people thought Dandridge was cold or arrogant, they misread her behavior. She was an introvert, so she needed time alone to regain her energy. Although Dandridge was shy, she was kind and never spoke negatively about people.

Many of Dandridge's scenes were quite physically demanding. At the beginning of the film, Carmen, a factory worker, is arrested for starting a vicious fight with another female factory worker. Joe, played by *Bright Road* costar Harry Belafonte, has to drive Carmen to the authorities. She refuses to cooperate. She laughs at Joe and teases him while he drives. Then, she makes her escape. She leaps from the open Jeep and hops onto a moving freight train. Joe runs after Carmen, chasing her as she leaps from car to car on the moving train. She jumps off, rolls down a ditch, and is captured by Joe, who ties her hands and feet and gags her mouth. Dandridge and Belafonte did their own stunts, even for this dangerous scene.

Preminger was thrilled with Dandridge's performance. He gave her cases of the best champagne, bought her expensive gifts, and began taking control of her life. He told her to wear only beige and white, so she did. He also took over her nightclub act, trying to make it more glamorous and theatrical. But Preminger's direction only hurt Dandridge's act.

Carmen's History

The movie *Carmen Jones* has a history that spans parts of two centuries. In 1827, Aleksander Pushkin, a black Russian poet, published "The Gypsies," a narrative poem about a gypsy girl, Zemfira, who brings to her camp her lover, Aleko, a Spanish soldier. Zemfira eventually grows tired of Aleko and takes another lover. Aleko murders her.

It seems likely that French writer Prosper Mérimée read a French translation of Pushkin's poem. In 1845, Mérimée published a novella titled *Carmen* that was strikingly similar to the story Pushkin told in "The Gypsies." Mérimée's *Carmen* then inspired French composer Georges Bizet to write and produce the 1875 comic opera *Carmen*. Initially, critics hated the opera because it broke many operatic traditions. Unfortunately, Bizet died of a heart attack in 1875 at age 36, just a few months after his *Carmen* opened and before it became one of the world's most popular operas.

In 1943, Oscar Hammerstein II adapted Bizet's *Carmen* by rewriting the lyrics, changing the setting to the present-day United States, and creating an all-black cast. He called the play *Carmen Jones*. Otto Preminger saw the stage production and thought he could improve it by adapting it to the screen.

Visiting with Cyril

While Dandridge was filming *Carmen Jones*, her father visited Los Angeles, but she did not want to see him. She was still angry with him, believing he had abandoned her as a child. Eager to see his daughter, Cyril got in touch with Geri. She realized that Cyril was not interested in seeing his daughter because she was famous. Geri said, "He wanted to explain that he didn't purposely dodge taking care of her as a child." Geri persuaded Dandridge to visit with her father, and they had a good talk one day. "I was a little more mature by then," said Dandridge.[6]

The two tried to change Dandridge's appearance, making her less seductive and more ladylike. "He was a bad influence," said Mills. "He was a great movie director, but he didn't know anything about nightclubs."[5]

After the filming of *Carmen Jones* wrapped, a flurry of publicity began. Dandridge was featured in photo shoots for magazines such as *Life, Ebony, Jet, Sepia*, and *Esquire*. That year, 1954, she became the first African-American woman to appear on the cover of *Life* magazine. Then, just before *Carmen Jones* was released in theaters, Dandridge suffered from more bouts of overwhelming anxiety. She was concerned that people might not like her performance. She also continued to worry about how the African-American community would react. In addition, Dandridge was irritated about how people often interpreted Carmen's character. Many of them—especially men—could

Preminger and Dandridge on the set of Porgy and Bess.

not see past Carmen's fiery beauty and believed her only interest was men. But to Dandridge, Carmen was much more: She was a strong, independent woman who would not allow any man to tell her what to do.

CARMEN'S POPULARITY

Carmen Jones opened on October 28, 1954. Photographers gathered outside the Rivoli Theater in New York that evening to get shots of all the stars,

Dandridge received an Oscar nomination for her performance in Carmen Jones.

especially Dandridge. Wearing a dazzling long white gown and jacket, she appeared to be completely happy.

After the premiere, Dandridge appeared on *The Tonight Show*, a late-night talk show, and then went to a party. The next morning, reviews of the movie appeared. Critics loved the movie and absolutely raved about the character of Carmen. People could not stop talking about Dandridge's beauty, acting skills, presence, and spirit. It seemed as though Preminger had been right: Dandridge was going to be a superstar.

The next few months were dizzying for Dandridge. Journalists begged for interviews and probed into her personal life. She was invited to the homes and parties of the most well-known celebrities in Hollywood and New York. People fawned over her. Dandridge responded by behaving like a queen. She acted so grand that Vivian and Geri were a little annoyed with her at times.

But in February 1955, when Dandridge heard her name announced as a nominee for the Best Actress Oscar, she ran to the telephone and called her mother and sister. The two sisters screamed with joy—and so did many of Dandridge's friends. One friend was so excited that he opened the windows and screamed Dandridge's name repeatedly. Because this was such a historic moment, several African-American newspapers published the story on their front pages.

Dandridge's Impact on the Civil Rights Movement

Status quo is a Latin term meaning "the way things are." In 1954, the US Supreme Court ruled in *Brown v. Board of Education* that educating black children and white children in "separate but equal" schools was unconstitutional. That decision struck down an 1896 ruling that permitted segregated schools, thus upsetting the status quo and launching the civil rights movement. Dandridge's rise to fame and recognition in 1954 seemed a good omen—and it gave hope to millions that racial equality would become the new status quo in the United States.

In her public statement responding to the nomination, Dandridge said,

[My] heart swelled with pride. . . . It is the first time a Negro performer in a leading role has ever won this distinction. It gives me courage to go on with my acting career. I hope that more Negro people will be employed in the motion picture industry.[7]

TOP OF THE WORLD

To capitalize on Dandridge's popularity, 20th Century Fox offered her a contract: She would make three films for the studio, which would pay her up to $125,000 per film. That was a lot of money in 1955. Although Dandridge had not yet received an offer to make a specific film, she was confident she would soon.

Nightclubs were also eager to have Dandridge appear, and they flooded her with requests to perform. The Last Frontier in Vegas, whose management had drained the pool to keep her from swimming, begged her to appear again. Dandridge broke yet another racial barrier when the most exclusive nightclub of all—the Empire Room at the Waldorf Hotel in New York City—booked her for a seven-week engagement. She was the first African American to stay and perform there, and she did not disappoint the hotel or its audiences.

In May, Dandridge took a short break from the Waldorf to travel to France for the Cannes Film Festival, an annual event that showcases new films. Hollywood's biggest movie stars and directors always attend. Dandridge, the first African American to attend the festival, won more cheers and applause from the European crowds than any of the white stars. The French went crazy for her, calling out "Dor-Tee! Dor-Tee!" whenever she appeared in public.[8]

After the festival, Dandridge returned to New York to finish her Waldorf engagement and to discuss some potential movie options. Although she had a contract to make three movies in the near future, no leading roles had been offered to her. However, she had been asked to play a supporting role in the upcoming movie *The King and I*. With Yul Brenner and Deborah Kerr as the stars, Dandridge would play Tuptim, a beautiful Burmese slave girl sent as a gift to the King of Siam. It was a good role, but it was not a lead role.

Dandridge agreed to play the part of Tuptim and began preparing for shooting. Although she felt hesitant about playing the part of a slave, she wanted the work. She also knew *The King and I* had the potential to be a huge hit. However, Preminger tried to talk her out of being in the film. He thought Dandridge was too big a star to play a supporting role, no matter how successful the movie might be. He argued that if Elizabeth Taylor or Marilyn Monroe had been nominated for an Oscar, she would accept nothing less than star status.

Earl Mills and Dandridge's other friends in the business disagreed with Preminger. They knew Dandridge deserved a better role, but they also knew Hollywood had a shortage of roles for African-American actresses. They thought Dandridge should make *The King and I* to stay in the public eye and to possibly attract more movie offers. But Dandridge gave in to Preminger and rejected the Tuptim role. She would have plenty of time later to regret her decision. ⌐

Dandridge in a publicity photo for Carmen Jones, 1954

Dandridge spoke to reporters after testifying in the criminal libel trial of Confidential *magazine in 1957.*

LANGUISHING IN HOLLYWOOD

epresentatives at 20th Century Fox were angry at Dandridge for backing out of the Tuptim role after she had agreed to make *The King and I*. Rita Moreno was given the part, and Dandridge got a reputation for being difficult. Producers and directors recognized Dandridge's outstanding talent and beauty, but they did not know what to do with her. They were afraid white audiences would not accept a black leading lady unless the film was originally intended to portray one. Many moviemakers told Dandridge they would love to have her star in a film when they found an appropriate role for her. So, Dandridge was repeatedly overlooked for roles she likely would have done well in simply because she was black.

When *The King and I* became a hit, winning nine Oscar nominations, Dandridge was sure she had made the wrong decision in backing out of the role of Tuptim. "Artistically, I started going downhill from that moment," she explained.[1] But Preminger refused to believe he might have been wrong about the role. He continued to lavish Dandridge with gifts, take her on shopping trips to Paris and New York, and show her off to his friends. Dandridge hoped he would propose marriage, but her friends knew better. Preminger wanted to own Dandridge. He was already married, and he would not jeopardize his career by marrying an African-American woman. Dandridge grew increasingly frustrated with their relationship, which ultimately ended.

When no movie roles came along, Dandridge
went back to saloon singing. During an engagement
at the Riviera Club in Las Vegas, she caught the eye
of the club's maître d', a white man named Jack
Denison. He became obsessed with Dandridge and
tried to get to know her. He sent her flowers, made
sure she got perfect room service, and kept staff from
serving food or drinks while Dandridge was singing
so she would not be disrupted. Denison finally met
Dandridge, but she was not impressed by him. He
continued flattering her, and she eventually got used
to him. He became a diversion for when she was
bored. He also helped distract her from thinking
about Preminger.

Now in her mid-thirties, Dandridge knew her
days as a movie star were numbered. Hollywood
had many leading roles for middle-aged men but not
for middle-aged women. Dandridge feared that if
she did not land a good movie deal soon, she might
be forgotten forever. In the meantime, she kept
on with her nightclub performances and often
took prescription tranquilizers and sleeping pills
to relax.

MOVIE JOBS

Even though Dandridge worried that she was getting too old to be a leading lady in Hollywood, she was offered movie work. In 1956, she made *Island in the Sun*, a film that featured an interracial romance. At the time, American films did not show a white character and a black character kissing or saying "I love you." Because of this restriction, the film's treatment of the interracial relationship was unrealistic. Dandridge grew increasingly frustrated with the story and her part

Confidential Lies

In 1957, Dandridge joined several other celebrities in suing the scandalous gossip magazine *Confidential* for libel. The publication was known for printing provocative articles that claimed to expose famous people's dirty little secrets.

Confidential had printed an article claiming knowledge of an affair Dandridge had with a "'pale' stranger in the woods" near Lake Tahoe, Nevada.[2] The man was a white band leader named Daniel Terry, and the article was titled "What Dorothy Dandridge Did in the Woods."[3]

In August 1957, Dandridge and other major stars testified in court. While on the witness stand, she told how racial mixing was not allowed in Lake Tahoe and that she had to obey this strict policy. She could not have taken a walk in the woods either by herself or with a white stranger, because she had to stay in her hotel suite most of the time. "Lake Tahoe at that time was very prejudiced," she explained. "Negroes were not permitted that freedom."[4] This was a well-known fact and actually benefited Dandridge in the lawsuit. She was awarded a $10,000 settlement in the case.

Actress Maureen O'Hara, left, speaks to Dandridge outside the libel trial against Confidential *magazine.*

in it. "I hated the part," she wrote to a friend.[5] She also hated the heat, the bugs, and the food while filming on location in the Caribbean on the islands of Barbados and Grenada.

In 1957, Dandridge made *Tamango*, a European movie. While this film focused on African slaves' fight for freedom, it also included an interracial romance. This caused the film to be banned in the United States. This was not an issue for European audiences. In fact, they were delighted with

Dandridge. While Dandridge filmed in France, she was followed by a throng of photographers and reporters wherever she went. Still, the film was also banned in the French colonies, including Algeria. Algeria was at war and the French government did not want to encourage additional uprisings by allowing the film to be seen.

Dandridge's next project was the low-budget 1958 film *The Decks Ran Red*. This American film included an interracial kiss, which was a newer occurrence in US films.

PORGY AND BESS

In 1958, Dandridge was offered a role in the film *Porgy and Bess*, which was based on a musical by George Gershwin. The story centers on a poor, disabled black man, Porgy, and a prostitute named Bess. There were some strong, admirable black characters in the script, but many characters were stereotypes. Like many in the African-American community, Dandridge was offended by the story's negative and stereotypical portrayals of black people. In 1958, the civil rights movement was well underway, and she did not want to be part of a film that might interfere with the progress of African Americans.

Several prominent black actors refused to work on the project. For example, Harry Belafonte and Cab Calloway would not participate. Diahann Carroll and Sidney Poitier also refused at first, but pressure from Samuel Goldwyn, the film's powerful producer, proved too much. They gave in against their better judgment. So did Dandridge.

The production of *Porgy and Bess* was plagued with problems. Finding the right singers to perform Dandridge and Poitier's songs proved difficult, so the singing was dubbed by opera singers. Then a fire destroyed the entire set—costumes, props, everything—at a cost of more than $2 million. Finally, the film's original director, Rouben Mamoulian, was fired and replaced by Otto Preminger, to Dandridge's great dismay.

From the first day of shooting, Preminger seemed to want to destroy Dandridge because of their

Behind the Mask

Many people noticed Dandridge's insecurity beneath her mask of elegance. She was terribly unhappy, but she still treated others with respect and kindness. One day, a young singer and dancer named Nichelle Nichols made a mistake and Preminger yelled at her. Dandridge gently took Nichols's hand and led her away, saying she knew the young dancer would be a big star someday. "The way she said that to me was delicate, beautiful, sensitive, compassionate," explained Nichols.[6] She held Dandridge in the highest regard after that.

past strained relationship. As she began reading her lines, he burst out, "What's the matter with you, Dorothy? You're supposed to be an actress."[7] He made her start again and then interrupted her, screaming that her acting was stupid. Feeling humiliated in front of the cast and crew, Dandridge crumbled. She was incapable of defending herself against Preminger. Every day, he screamed at her until she dissolved into tears and fled the set. Then he criticized her for being unable to take criticism. He was unkind to the rest of the cast, as well, but he seemed to save his worst tirades for Dandridge.

Longing for Love

Porgy and Bess provided work for Dandridge, but she longed for love. If only the right man would come along, she could get married and give up show business. More than anything else, she wanted to be a

Besting the Beast

One day on the set of *Porgy and Bess,* the cast asked for a meeting with Preminger. They had endured enough of his cruelty and disrespect and wanted to let him know that. Dandridge had the day off and knew nothing about the meeting. According to cast member Nichelle Nichols, "The actors ate him alive. He knew he had a mutiny on his hands."[8] The actors demanded he treat them all with more respect, especially Dandridge. His poor treatment of her demoralized all of them. After the meeting, Preminger toned down his behavior and became more respectful.

Tamango

The film *Tamango* is set on a slave ship in the early 1800s. Dandridge's character, a slave mistress belonging to the ship's captain, must choose to remain loyal to her white master or join her people in a revolt against their captors led by a slave named Tamango. In the end, she chooses to fight alongside her own people. Released in August 1959, at a time when the civil rights movement was gaining strength, *Tamango* was much more in line with the mood of the movement than was *Porgy and Bess*—a story that many viewed as damaging efforts at achieving equality for African Americans.

wife who was loved and cherished. Unfortunately, most of the men she had dated were white and unwilling to marry an African-American woman.

Denison had continued pursuing Dandridge, flattering her and boasting of his ability to take care of her. When the two began dating, Dandridge's friends warned her about him, saying he was only after her money. Dandridge did not listen to her friends or to her own intuition. She had seen Denison's bad side but had chosen to ignore the warning signs. He had a violent temper and had threatened to kill her on at least one occasion. Still, Dandridge married Denison on June 23, 1959. It was the biggest mistake of her life.

Dandridge in a promotional photo for Island in the Sun

Jack Denison and Dandridge, circa 1959

Catch a Fallen Star

andridge decided to marry again in 1959 with the hope that she would at last feel loved and appreciated. But she soon realized that Denison was a con artist. Dandridge had given him $150,000 to run a restaurant, and it had failed. He had not married her for love. He simply wanted to use her and her money.

Denison isolated Dandridge from her friends and took control of her life. He said he would manage her career and made her fire her loyal friend and agent, Earl Mills. Although Dandridge was worried about money, she sold her lovely home and bought a bigger, fancier home to please her husband. Having to work harder than ever to support herself, her daughter, and her husband, she continued singing in nightclubs. She also costarred in the 1960 movie *Malaga*, which was disappointing to her in many ways.

Being married to Denison was a nightmare for Dandridge. He started hitting her. At first, it was one slap, so Dandridge forgave him. But then the physical and verbal abuse became more vicious and more frequent. To escape the physical and emotional pain, Dandridge began drinking heavily and taking pills. She often seemed unfocused and disoriented, which affected her work. Her nightclub performances began to lose their brilliance. For several months, she retreated from the spotlight.

On many occasions, Dandridge's Hollywood contacts approached her about being in movies, which excited the performer. However, the discussions led nowhere. Dandridge made guest appearances on television dramas and game shows, but taking such jobs signaled her decline. At the time, movie stars did not make these kinds of appearances unless they were desperate for work.

Crushed

Dandridge's financial problems worsened, as did her husband's behavior. Twice, she asked him to leave, but he refused to go. He raged through the house, breaking crystal and china and shredding the linens. He even stole her jewelry and sold it at a pawnshop.

Dandridge filed for divorce in 1962, and a Los Angeles court ordered Denison to leave her house. He did, but he left her deeply in debt and emotionally and physically devastated. The bank foreclosed on her house, and she was forced to declare bankruptcy. But her most crushing loss was yet to come.

With her finances in ruins, Dandridge could no longer afford to pay Helen Calhoun to care for Lynn. Feeling she had no other choice, Dandridge surrendered her parental rights and committed Lynn to a state institution. In Dandridge's mind, her life was a complete failure. Once again, she coped with the situation with alcohol and medication. In her words,

> *That collapse of fortune left me as bewildered a human being as you could find. Not knowing which way to turn, . . . desiring death more than anything else, I took pills. Pills to pep myself up, pills to slow myself down.* [1]

Dandridge continued drinking and slid deeper into depression. In desperation, she agreed to write her autobiography for the publisher Bernard Geis and signed a contract for $10,000. Dandridge's friends—especially Geri—believed she was being taken advantage of by the publisher and were horrified. Dandridge recorded tapes to be used in writing the book, and rumor spread that copies of her tapes were being played and sold at Hollywood parties, where guests would listen to the recordings and joke about Dandridge.

Dandridge's friends continued to be deeply concerned about her state of mind. She was so fragile that

The Autobiography

Everything and Nothing: The Dorothy Dandridge Tragedy is Dandridge's autobiography. It was published in 1970. It was coauthored by Earl Conrad.

she seemed like a lost and frightened child. In her loneliness, Dandridge sometimes wandered around her neighborhood. At other times, she sat in cafés. At one point, she was hospitalized, where she met with a psychiatrist.

COMEBACK ROAD

Despite Dandridge's self-destructive behavior, she still found hope. In 1965, she contacted Earl Mills, her old friend and former manager, and asked him to help her make a comeback. He agreed.

Dandridge began rehearsing music, exercising, and limiting her consumption of alcohol and pills. She accepted every job offer that came her way—no matter how small. Four days before she was scheduled to perform in New York in September, Mills received a call from Raul Fernandez, a Mexican film producer who was interested in hiring Dandridge. Mills took Dandridge to Mexico to meet Fernandez, who signed the star to a two-film contract for $100,000.

While Dandridge was in Mexico, her foot began hurting. Mills took her to a doctor for an X-ray, which revealed a small fracture. It had happened a few days earlier, when Dandridge had twisted her ankle while walking down a flight of stairs. The injury seemed a small setback, but Dandridge worried that having her foot in a cast would hurt her upcoming performance in New York.

A Tragic Loss

Dandridge returned to her apartment in Los Angeles on September 7, 1965, and began packing for her trip to New York. Mills had arranged to pick her up the next morning. Dandridge had difficulty unwinding that night and made several telephone calls to friends and family.

The next morning, Mills telephoned Dandridge. When she did not answer, he went to her apartment. Dandridge did not answer the door and it was chained, so he left. Mills returned two hours later. When Dandridge still did not appear, he finally broke open the

Cyril's Last Visit

Cyril Dandridge saw his daughter Dorothy about a year before her death. When the two met, Dorothy let her father try to make up for being absent during her childhood. That was the last time Cyril saw her. When he arrived in Los Angeles to attend his daughter's funeral, he learned that it had taken place days earlier. Ruby, his ex-wife, had purposely told Cyril the wrong date.

door. Mills found Dandridge lying on the bathroom floor, curled on her side like a sleeping child. She wore only a blue scarf on her head and was cold to the touch. She was dead at the age of 42. She had left a note:

> *In case of my death—to whomever discovers it—don't remove anything I have on—scarf, gown or underwear—Cremate me right away—If I have anything, money, furniture, give to my mother Ruby Dandridge—She will know what to do.* [2]

Dandridge's death was announced on radio and television news programs and in newspaper headlines. The coroner's report stated that she died of an overdose of antidepressants. It was impossible to determine if the overdose had been intentional or accidental. Mills and many of Dandridge's friends and family refused to believe her death was suicide. Dandridge had been in a good mood when Mills had seen her the day before. She was determined to make a comeback.

But Geri was not as certain. Dandridge had attempted suicide in the past and had expressed doubts about her comeback. Also, some six months before her death, Dandridge had sent notes to Mills and Geri about what to do if she were ever found dead. Accidental or not, it seemed she knew her life would end this way.

A private service was held for family and friends at Little Chapel of the Flowers, located at Forest Lawn Cemetery in Glendale, a suburb of Los Angeles. Her ashes are entombed at the cemetery's Freedom Mausoleum.

REDISCOVERING DANDRIDGE

Following Dandridge's death, the newspapers published many stories about her. But with time, her image faded from public memory. Unlike white stars who had died at a young age, such as Marilyn Monroe and James Dean,

Separated Sisters

Dorothy and Vivian Dandridge were very close, but they were competitive, too. Ruby obviously favored Dorothy, especially when she became a star. Vivian tried to be supportive of her sister, but over the years, Dorothy became more demanding of Vivian's time and attention. Dorothy did not seem to understand that Vivian had her own life.

As an adult, Vivian became closer to their father, while Dorothy grew closer to their mother. As Vivian learned the truth about her parents, she had more conflicts with her mother—and with Dorothy, too.

Although Dorothy was known for her sweet and gracious ways, she had another side that she expressed only to Vivian. Perhaps Dorothy thought she could get away with treating her sister badly at times—but she was wrong.

Vivian dropped out of Dorothy's life in the late 1950s and never saw Dorothy again. Even though Vivian grieved deeply when Dorothy died, she did not attend her sister's funeral. Vivian Dandridge died in 1991. She was living in Seattle, Washington, at the time of her death. She was 70 years old.

Actress Halle Berry celebrates her 2000 Golden Globe win for her role in Introducing Dorothy Dandridge.

Dandridge did not become more popular after she died.

Then, one day in the mid-1980s, a 19-year-old girl named Halle Berry saw the movie *Carmen Jones* on television. She could not understand why she had never heard of Dandridge before. Berry explained,

> *I was mesmerized by her poise and her charisma. I had never seen a Black woman quite like that in a film. She was someone I could admire and aspire to be like. She gave me hope.*[3]

Berry soon became a Hollywood star and was determined to bring Dandridge's life story to the screen. Berry wanted the world to know and remember this remarkable woman. In 1999, Berry produced and starred in the HBO movie *Introducing Dorothy Dandridge*. She won several awards for her portrayal of Dandridge, including an Emmy and a Golden Globe. Geri thought highly of Berry's portrayal, saying,

> She absolutely stole the essence of Dottie and she truly understood her. I felt like, for two hours, I'd been visiting with Dottie again. She would have been so pleased, so happy.[4]

The success of the movie *Introducing Dorothy Dandridge* has helped keep Dandridge's story alive. Dandridge also became important as a role model for Berry, who noted,

> She blazed a trail for Black actresses and fought so hard to widen horizons for

Ruby's Success

Ruby Dandridge was never a leading actor, but she played small parts in radio, movies, and television shows. With her high, squeaky voice, she was often cast as a comical maid. Whenever Ruby started talking, audiences usually started laughing.

Ruby was well known for her roles in the *Amos 'n' Andy* programs and the 1950s television show *Beulah*, starring Hattie McDaniel. Ruby also did cartoon voices for racially stereotyped "mammy" characters—cartoons that are now censored as unacceptably bigoted.

Ruby Dandridge died of a heart attack in 1987 at the age of 87. Her ashes are entombed next to Dorothy's.

our people. That's how I approach my career. I want to fight as hard as she did.[5]

Dandridge was an African-American woman who lived during a particularly challenging time for African Americans across the country, including Hollywood. Her talent did not make her exempt from racism and discrimination, but it did give her opportunities to fight these issues.

Dandridge is an icon for aspiring African-American actresses, but she is also much more. Her life was one of success and failure, struggle and determination. She met personal and professional challenges and continued to push forward in pursuit of her dreams. Dorothy Dandridge is an inspiration for all people, regardless of race, sex, or aspiration.

Walk of Fame

After Dandridge's death, many of her friends worked to keep her memory alive. Harry Belafonte and others campaigned to have a star placed for her on the Walk of Fame in Hollywood. Finally, on January 18, 1984, almost 20 years after her death, Dandridge's star was unveiled in a ceremony that honored her life and work.

*Dandridge paved the way for African-American actresses in Hollywood,
though her life can serve as inspiration to anyone.*

TIMELINE

1922

Dorothy Dandridge is born in Cleveland, Ohio, on November 9.

1934

The Dandridge Sisters win a singing contest in Los Angeles, California.

1937

The Dandridge Sisters film *A Day at the Races*.

1942

Dandridge and Harold Nicholas marry on September 6.

1943

Dandridge gives birth to a daughter, Harolyn Suzanne Nicholas, on September 1.

1949

Dandridge files for divorce from Nicholas, enrolls in the Actor's Lab, and begins working to become a nightclub singer.

1938	**1939**	**1941**
The Dandridge Sisters film *Going Places.* They open at the Cotton Club in New York City on September 28.	In June, the Dandridge Sisters begin their singing tour in Europe. Later that year, Dandridge decides to begin her solo career.	On July 10, the stage musical *Jump for Joy* opens, starring Dandridge.

1949	**1951**	**1951**
Dandridge opens at the Bingo, a supper club in Las Vegas, Nevada.	Dandridge is featured on the cover of *Ebony* magazine's April issue.	Dandridge makes *Tarzan's Peril* and *The Harlem Globetrotters.*

TIMELINE

1952	1954	1954
Dandridge lands a costarring role in *Bright Road*.	Dandridge makes *Carmen Jones*.	Dandridge becomes the first African-American woman to grace the cover of *Life* magazine.

1956	1957	1958
Dandridge makes *Island in the Sun*.	Dandridge makes *Tamango*.	Dandridge makes *Porgy and Bess*.

1955

1955

1955

Dandridge is the first African American to be nominated for the Best Actress Oscar for her performance in *Carmen Jones.*

Dandridge becomes the first African-American woman to present an Academy Award.

On April 11, Dandridge opens in the Empire Room at the Waldorf Hotel in New York City.

1959

1962

1965

Dandridge marries Jack Denison on June 23.

Dandridge divorces Denison.

While starting to make a comeback, Dandridge is found dead on September 8.

Essential Facts

Date of Birth
November 9, 1922

Place of Birth
Cleveland, Ohio

Date of Death
September 8, 1965

Parents
Cyril and Ruby Dandridge

Education
Homeschooled and some public education

Marriages
Harold Nicholas (1942–1951); Jack Denison (1959–1962)

Children
Harolyn Suzanne Nicholas

Career Highlights
Dandridge began working as an entertainer when she was very young, performing as part of the Wonder Children and then the

Dandridge Sisters, entertaining audiences at New York's Cotton Club and in Europe. Later, Dandridge performed solo, singing in nightclubs. She also had a movie career that peaked in 1954, when she starred in *Carmen Jones* and became the first African-American woman to be nominated for a Best Actress Oscar.

SOCIETAL CONTRIBUTION

Throughout her career, Dandridge challenged racism. As a successful African-American entertainer, she provided hope for other African Americans that the racial divide was growing smaller. She also provided a role model for young African-American women, in particular, who dreamed of becoming professional actors.

CONFLICTS

As an African American living during a time when segregation was the norm and racism was constant, Dandridge faced both personal and professional challenges. She was sometimes restricted from staying at the same hotels and using the same bathrooms, pools, and other facilities as white people. In addition, she was considered unsuitable for marriage by several white men with whom she had serious relationships. As an actress, Dandridge was passed over for movie roles for which she was clearly well qualified.

QUOTE

"[My] heart swelled with pride. . . . It is the first time a Negro performer in a leading role has ever won this distinction. It gives me courage to go on with my acting career. I hope that more Negro people will be employed in the motion picture industry."—*Dorothy Dandridge, on being nominated for an Oscar*

Glossary

antidepressant
A prescribed medicine that helps someone feel less depressed or anxious.

bigotry
An attitude of narrow-mindedness and intolerance, especially regarding a certain group of people.

color barrier
Social barriers that keep blacks from participating in activities with whites.

coroner
An official who investigates unexplained deaths.

dialect
A special variety of a language that has unique pronunciations, structure, and grammar from the standard language.

gig
A scheduled performance by one or more musicians, such as a singer or band.

hyperventilate
To breathe too rapidly, causing faintness or dizziness.

languish
To be ignored or neglected.

libel
The act of writing or printing a statement that is false and damages a person's reputation.

maître d'
The master of a hotel, restaurant, or nightclub.

mesmerize
To hypnotize or put under a spell.

NAACP
National Association for the Advancement of Colored Persons is a US organization dedicated to helping African Americans receive equal treatment in society.

oxygen deprivation
> The condition of not getting enough oxygen, which is necessary for proper functioning; a lack of oxygen often results in some type of impairment.

poise
> Grace, elegance.

prestigious
> Important, popular.

provocative
> Attractive, appealing.

segregation
> The separation or isolation of certain groups based on a characteristic such as race or ethnicity, skin color, or social class.

stereotype
> A prejudiced idea or attitude about a certain group of people.

subservient
> Inferior, subordinate.

tirade
> A vicious or angry lecture.

ADDITIONAL RESOURCES

SELECTED BIBLIOGRAPHY

Bogle, Donald. *Dorothy Dandridge: A Biography*. New York: Amistad, 1997. Print.

Dandridge, Dorothy, and Earl Conrad. *Everything and Nothing: The Dorothy Dandridge Tragedy*. New York: HarperCollins, 2000. Print.

Mills, Earl. *Dorothy Dandridge: An Intimate Biography*. Los Angeles, CA: Holloway, 1999. Print.

FURTHER READINGS

Gates, Henry Louis, Jr., and Evelyn Brooks Higenbotham, eds. *African American Lives*. New York: Oxford UP, 2004. Print.

Mapp, Edward. *African Americans and the Oscar: Decades of Struggle and Achievement*. Lanham, MD: Scarecrow, 2008. Print.

Potter, Joan. *African American Firsts: Famous Little-known and Unsung Triumphs of Blacks in America*. New York: Dafina, 2002. Print.

Regester, Charlene. *African American Actresses: The Struggle for Visibility, 1900–1960*. Bloomington, IN: Indiana UP, 2010. Print.

WEB LINKS

To learn more about Dorothy Dandridge, visit ABDO Publishing Company online at **www.abdopublishing.com**. Web sites about Dorothy Dandridge are featured on our Book Links page. These links are routinely monitored and updated to provide the most current information available.

Places to Visit

Freedom Mausoleum
Forest Lawn Cemetery, Glendale, 1712 South Glendale Avenue
Glendale, CA 91205
1-800-204-3131
www.forestlawn.com/About-Forest-Lawn/Glendale-Freedom-Mausoleum.asp
Dandridge's ashes are entombed at the mausoleum. The cemetery also has a second mausoleum, as well as multiple chapels, a sculpture garden, and a flower shop.

Hollywood Walk of Fame
6721 Hollywood Boulevard, Hollywood, CA 90028
www.hollywoodchamber.net/index.php?page=7
Dandridge's star is located three tiles from the curb, facing west.

National Museum of African American History and Culture
Smithsonian Institution, National Museum of American History, Capital Gallery, 600 Maryland Avenue SW, Suite 7001
Washington, DC 20013-7012
www.nmaahc.si.edu
Collections highlight the breadth and depth of African-American culture and history. Exhibits highlight New York's famous Apollo Theater and the role of visual images in the civil rights movement.

Source Notes

Chapter 1. A Symbol of Hope

1. "Nicholl Fellowships in Screenwriting." *Oscars.org*. The Academy of Motion Picture Arts and Sciences, 2010. Web. 5 Apr. 2010.

2. Edward Mapp. *African Americans and the Oscar: Decades of Struggle and Achievement*. Lanham, MD: Scarecrow, 2008. 139. Print.

3. Kwakiutl L. Dreher. *Dancing on the White Page: Black Women Entertainers Writing Autobiography*. Albany, NY: SUNY, 2008. 192. Print.

4. Earl Mills. *Dorothy Dandridge: An Intimate Biography*. Los Angeles, CA: Holloway, 1999. 11. Print.

5. Edward Mapp. *African Americans and the Oscar: Decades of Struggle and Achievement*. Lanham, MD: Scarecrow, 2008. 94. Print.

Chapter 2. Wonder Child

1. Donald Bogle. *Dorothy Dandridge: A Biography*. New York: Amistad, 1997. 9. Print.

2. Ibid. 14.

3. Paul Laurence Dunbar. "In the Morning." *Dunbar.org*. University of Dayton, 3 Feb. 2003. Web. 1 Sept. 2010.

Chapter 3. California Girl

1. Donald Bogle. *Dorothy Dandridge: A Biography*. New York: Amistad, 1997. 71. Print.

2. Ibid. 57.

3. Rusty Frank. *Tap: The Greatest Tap Dance Stars and Their Stories, 1900–1955*. New York: Da Capo, 1994. 66. Print.

4. Ibid. 70.

Chapter 4. Mrs. Nicholas

1. Donald Bogle. *Dorothy Dandridge: A Biography*. New York: Amistad, 1997. 80. Print.

2. Giles Milton. "Jump for Joy." *The Cannonball Adderley Rendezvous*. N.p., n.d. Web. 1 Sept. 2010.

3. Donald Bogle. *Dorothy Dandridge: A Biography*. New York: Amistad, 1997. 91. Print.

Chapter 5. Starting Over

1. Donald Bogle. *Dorothy Dandridge: A Biography*. New York: Amistad, 1997. 18. Print.

2. Dorothy Dandridge and Earl Conrad. *Everything and Nothing: The Dorothy Dandridge Tragedy*. New York: HarperCollins, 2000. 218.

3. Donald Bogle. *Dorothy Dandridge: A Biography*. New York: Amistad, 1997. 184. Print.

4. Ibid. 157.

5. Ibid. 177.

Chapter 6. A Rising Star

1. Donald Bogle. *Dorothy Dandridge: A Biography*. New York: Amistad, 1997. 237. Print.

2. Ibid. 237–238.

3. Ibid. 246.

4. Ibid. 240.

5. Ibid. 241.

6. Ibid. 258.

7. Geoffrey MacNab. "Otto Preminger: The Method in His Madness." *The Independent Online*. Independent Print Limited, 2010. Web. 12 May 2010.

8. Donald Bogle. *Dorothy Dandridge: A Biography*. New York: Amistad, 1997. 271. Print.

9. Ibid. 273.

10. Ibid. 376.

Chapter 7. The First African-American Movie Star

1. Donald Bogle. *Dorothy Dandridge: A Biography*. New York: Amistad, 1997. 274. Print.

2. Ibid. 281.

3. Ibid. 280.

4. Ibid. 276.

5. Ibid. 319.

6. Ibid. 291.

7. Ibid. 320.

8. Ibid. 331.

Source Notes Continued

Chapter 8. Languishing in Hollywood

1. Donald Bogle. *Dorothy Dandridge: A Biography*. New York: Amistad, 1997. 355. Print.

2. Ibid. 375.

3. Douglas O. Linder. "The Confidential Magazine Trial: An Account." *Famous Trials*. University of Missouri–Kansas City School of Law. n.d. Web. 1 Sept. 2010.

4. Ibid.

5. Donald Bogle. *Dorothy Dandridge: A Biography*. New York: Amistad, 1997. 360. Print.

6. Ibid. 415.

7. Ibid. 413.

8. Ibid. 420.

Chapter 9. Catch a Fallen Star

1. Donald Bogle. *Dorothy Dandridge: A Biography*. New York: Amistad, 1997. 506. Print.

2. Donald Bogle. "The Last Days of Dorothy Dandridge." *Ebony* August 1997: 64. Print.

3. "Halle Berry Brings the Passion and Pain of Dorothy Dandridge to HBO Movie." *Jet* 23 Aug. 1999: 61. Print.

4. Laura B. Randolph. "Halle Berry: On How She Found Dorothy Dandridge's Spirit—and Finally Healed Her Own." *Ebony* Aug. 1999: 98. Print.

5. Ibid. 94.

INDEX

INDEX CONTINUED

About the Author

DeAnn Herringshaw has been working as a writer, editor, and writing consultant for educational and non-profit organizations for more than 15 years. Her favorite projects include writing a section of a book on homelessness, doing public speaking on mental health, and writing this biography, her first book. She especially enjoys doing research, because she loves the challenge of learning and sharing new ideas. DeAnn is a former horse trainer and riding instructor and volunteers for a therapeutic riding program for handicapped children and adults. She is a mother of four and lives in St. Paul, Minnesota, with her youngest son.

Photo Credits

Photofest, cover, 3, 20, 34, 40, 68, 84, 95, 96 (bottom), 98 (top), 99; Marty Lederhandler/AP Images, 6; AP Images, 11, 13, 24, 30, 33, 44, 52, 61, 97; Miller Studio/Library of Congress, 14, 96 (top); John Vachon/Library of Congress, 23; Twentieth Century-Fox Film Corporation/Photofest, 37; Matt Rourke/ AP Images, 43; Ed Ford/AP Images, 51; Tony Dejak/AP Images, 59; AP Images, File, 62; Columbia Pictures /Photofest, 67; 20th Century-Fox/Photofest, 73; Harold Filan/AP Images, 74, 78, 98 (bottom); Hulton Archive/Getty Images, 83; Kevork Djansezian/ AP Images, 92